THE SEASONS OF VEUVE CLICQUOT

A SOCIAL COOKBOOK FOR ALL CELEBRATIONS

STÉPHANE GERSCHEL

RIZZOLI
NEW YORK

First published in the United States of America in 2011 by
RIZZOLI INTERNATIONAL PUBLICATIONS, INC.
300 Park Avenue South
New York, NY 10010
www.rizzoliusa.com

ISBN-13: 978-0-8478-3693-2
Library of Congress Control Number: 2011935929
© 2011 Rizzoli International Publications, Inc.
© 2011 Stéphane Gerschel
Texts © 2011 by their authors

Art Director: Duncan Campbell
Editor: Catherine Bonifassi

Printed and bound in China

THE SEASONS OF VEUVE CLICQUOT

A SOCIAL COOKBOOK FOR ALL CELEBRATIONS

STÉPHANE GERSCHEL

Foreword by Sir Elton John & David Furnish

EDITED BY ELENA LUOTO MEISTER

RIZZOLI
NEW YORK

New York · Paris · London · Milan

CONTENTS

L'scalier des millesimes, "the staircase of vintages." The years when the harvest is particularly good and yields wines of exceptional quality are recognized by Champagne houses, who then declare a vintage year to the local authorities.

365

DAYS TO CELEBRATE WITH VEUVE CLICQUOT

Foreword by Sir Elton John & David Furnish

Our lives—both public and private—testify to the fact that we don't exactly go by the book. Not to mention that, whether in music, film, or life, we live to entertain others.

We enjoy the story of the widow Clicquot, who two centuries ago decided to go against everything that had been previously written and drew up her own path. Daringly, she broke the mold and made the drink of the gods more widely available for celebrating special moments.

We thank the people who perpetuate her legacy today, and their commitment to the Elton John AIDS Foundation, because their dedication to live in style, season after season, does not prevent them from understanding that part of enjoying life is to give back to those in need.

INTRODUCTION

Celebrating the Seasons with Veuve Clicquot

It is a lucky thing that Veuve Clicquot and the Season found one another, as otherwise social life would never be what it is now. Social calendars turn by Season events—Great Britain's Goodwood Revival in autumn, Brazil's Carnaval in winter, Milan Design Week in spring, the New York Polo Classic in summer—to name just a few. Naturally, Champagne is the celebratory drink for festivities of such renown. And Veuve Clicquot has become the only Champagne for the Season across the world embodying the lifestyle of sophistication, luxury, and taste. It is this quality that led me to write this book.

The Season, like Veuve Clicquot, has been around for centuries. It was born in England, a country built on tradition. Many of the Season events such as Royal Ascot, Wimbledon, and Henley, have been in place for centuries; meanwhile they have been joined by newer events such as horse racing at the Cheltenham Gold Cup or music concerts at the Hampton Court Palace Festival.

The social season, referred to by those in the know as "the Season," first arose from London's seventeenth-century elite and reached its peak in the nineteenth century. Comprised principally of aristocratic landowning families, the British elite would often regard their country houses as their principal homes. These families would, however, spend several months of the year in London to socialize and engage in politics. In London, the most exclusive events were held at town mansions of leading members of the aristocracy, events

that formed the basis of the Season. By no coincidence, the Season generally coincided with the sitting of Parliament, which traditionally began around Easter and ended with the "Glorious Twelfth" (August 12), the start of the red grouse shooting season. After the First World War many aristocratic families gave up their London mansions, and the traditional version of the Season began to decline. Since then, a more inclusive and worldly version has taken its place.

The Season today is enjoyed in locations as wide-ranging as Shanghai, Saint Petersburg, and Chicago. Celebrating the Season has always meant "seeing and being seen," but it is much more. There is always a centerpiece to a Season event, an activity that is a compelling reason to gather. From yacht races to film festivals the Season is what to do as well as whom to do it with.

Of course, the sparkle of the Season festivities pair naturally with Veuve Clicquot Champagne. Veuve Clicquot imagined reviving the traditional concept of "see and be seen" amid a collection of quality events that would extend the world round. *Quality* is the operative word here, as the Season events partnered with Veuve Clicquot are the most high-profile social activities in the world.

Since becoming the Veuve Clicquot Season, the various Season events have evolved, modernized, and expanded in repertoire. Veuve Clicquot has put its Yellow spin on the Season to make events more contemporary,

Top hats and scorekeeping at Ascot.

modern, and audacious. Instead of ignoring the rules of Season tradition, Veuve Clicquot has simply reinvented them.

Worldwide, Veuve Clicquot Champagne is known as a brand of distinction. And although Champagne is intended to toast the exceptional occasion, we at Veuve Clicquot believe an occasion can be created daily. Veuve Clicquot sponsors an event every single day—there are at least 365 celebratory occasions in the year. The Champagne Season is thriving!

As farming is at the heart of both my family and vocation, my father having farmed his whole life and left the family estate to me to manage, I know full well that wine is, after all, an agricultural product wholly dependent on the seasons. The spring budding of the vines, the summer growth, the autumn harvest—Veuve Clicquot Champagne is as connected to the seasons of the field as it is to the timetables of the cellars. Seasons are milestones for us that denote the precise steps for winemaking and vineyard tending.

It is because of this connection to nature and the earth that Veuve Clicquot has made a conscientious stand in regards to caring for our precious natural resources, taking environmental awareness to a level unmatched by our peers. Veuve Clicquot wants to do its share to promote responsible and sustainable growth. This has become the company commitment.

Environmental awareness has long been instilled as a value at Veuve Clicquot and, most importantly, has become a resolute practice: for twenty years, we have been engaged in integrated viticulture; we use recycled paper and FSC-certified packaging; we are developing a bottle that is 15 percent lighter and so more ecological; we have become the champions of "sexual confusion" (a funny name for a way to manage insects without the use of pesticides); we've renewed our ISO certification 14001 (an international standard of environmental commitment); we are the first Champagne house to achieve its carbon footprint objective since the goal was set in 2002; we've reduced our water consumption by half over the past five years; and we sort 97 percent of our waste. In short, Veuve Clicquot is taking action.

Environmentally conscious actions come in many forms. For example, an individual can choose seasonal and local foods and therefore diminish both wasteful

Pinot Noir grapes at a Veuve Clicquot harvest in the 1970s. Pinot Noir is the backbone of the full-bodied Veuve Clicquot Champagnes, accounting for as much as 55 percent of the La Grande Dame blend.

A present from Veuve Clicquot to His Serene
Highness Prince Rainier III of Monaco, shortly
before his marriage in 1956. The vintage
1929 was the birth year of princess-to-be and
Hollywood star Grace Kelly.

transportation costs and emissions and dangerous pesticide use. Seasonal eating has become a trend of late, as more and more people recognize that it is the more ethical and delicious way to dine. By no coincidence, the selection of recipes for this book concentrates on seasonal cuisine, some of them being my own family recipes from our region of southwest France.

The recipes reveal the dual purpose of this book: to relive the exciting events of the Veuve Clicquot Season and dine on the Champagne cuisine that accompanies the fun, and to learn what delicacies to serve at which occasion or what finger food is best for a party of sixty. From gourmet dinners to harvest picnics, *A Social Cookbook* provides the recipe while Veuve Clicquot Champagne provides the refreshment. One final note on Champagne and this book, as the former has become my passion and the latter its outlet: I continue to be fascinated by how much there is to know about Champagne—my education continues daily. But

the most basic premise of Champagne is that it is a wine best enjoyed with food. Food pairing is just as important to Champagne enjoyment as it is to any other variety of wine. Often we enjoy a white Burgundy with our fish or a glass of Sauternes with pudding, familiar as we are with how each course pairs best with its own wine selection. Food pairing with Champagne follows the same principle: for the full *dégustation* experience, each course of a meal is best enjoyed with its own Champagne complement.

Furthermore, through the Champagne experiences depicted in this book, one discovers not only how food can be exquisitely paired with Champagne, but also how Champagne has its own sophisticated, distinctive place at the table. This, above all, prompted me to write and share the joy of Champagne.

Cheers!

AUTUMN

AUTUMN

The calendar year begins in autumn for the winemaker, when the season yields the year's harvest: a new wine. This is a key moment in Champagne, the northernmost wine region in France, as the grapes have finally matured enough to be harvested and then pressed and separated into vats by vineyard and grape variety. This beginning of the winemaking process is the natural starting point for the vineyard as well as for the Champagne season.

CHAMPAGNE MAKING

Autumn Harvest

Autumn is a return to schedules and timetables after the rejuvenating summer sunshine. But autumn is also a festive time of thanksgiving for nature's bounty and a nostalgic look at the past with imagery of smiling vineyard workers with *hottes de vendange*, the grape-collecting baskets, strapped to their backs. These baskets are such a powerful symbol of bountiful gifts that in France even Santa, in the deep of winter, wears one of these baskets to carry his gifts.

The autumn is a joyful season at Veuve Clicquot as well, as we host VIP parties in the vineyards to celebrate our new year and its newest wine, giving thanks for the cornucopia of autumn harvest.

Wine is a symbol of happiness but also of health—up until the twentieth century people largely drank wine, as water could be unclean and laden with bacteria. I once saw a menu from about 120 years ago, detailing the dishes and accompanying wines for a fifteen-course meal (not uncommon for a celebration at that time). Food and wine pairings abounded—a Bordeaux with the cheese, for example—but what struck me was a small sentence on the bottom of the menu: "Beaujolais servi en fraîcheur pendant tout le repas." Translation: "A chilled Beaujolais would

be served throughout the meal, alongside the other wine pairings, in lieu of water." True, the wine back then had a lower alcohol concentration, but this was a reminder for me of how integral wine has been and still is to French homes. The history of food and wine drinking extends to food and winemaking. In centuries past, harvest meant hard, physical work for the winemakers. One had to rise before the sun and work the vineyards, harvesting by hand, until a short break midmorning. Then it was back to work until about half past noon, when the extreme heat of the midday sun would force the workers to quit for the day. After such exertion, the harvesters would return home, ravenous, to enjoy a delicious *potée Champenoise*, or "harvester's meal." The *potée Champenoise* has become a regional specialty, a sort of stew rich with vegetables and meats. As the harvesters would typically only eat this one meal, it needed to be hearty in order to sustain them for the work that would begin again the next day.

Veuve Clicquot has put its gourmet twist on this old favorite, a *potée Champenoise* to sustain the most ravenous yet cultivated of appetites.

Extremely labor-intensive, the harvest in Champagne is still to this day done entirely by hand.

Harvesters in a horse-drawn carriage, c. 1970.

Past and present: fifty years separate these two pictures, yet the gestures are still the same.

THE HARVESTER'S MEAL

LA POTÉE CHAMPENOISE

INGREDIENTS (serves 8):

2¼ pounds of lightly salted bacon in one piece
1 head green cabbage
1 pound pork shoulder
4 carrots
4 turnips
2¼ pounds of potatoes
8 smoked sausages, such as kielbasa
1 thick slice smoked ham
Salt and freshly ground black pepper to taste

Put the bacon in a bowl and cover with cold water; soak in the refrigerator overnight to remove excess salt.

Cut the cabbage into quarters, cook in a pot of simmering water for 10 minutes, then drain and set aside.

Put the bacon and pork shoulder in a pressure cooker with 3 quarts water. Close the pressure cooker and boil for 15 minutes. Add the carrots, turnips, and cabbage and cook for 15 minutes. Add the potatoes, sausages, and ham and cook for 12 minutes. Add salt and pepper as needed. Serve in soup plates.

The *potée Champenoise* as prepared by Veuve Clicquot's chefs at the Manoir de Verzy.

Shooting in France happens from dawn to the end of morning and is traditionally followed by a much-awaited feast which can be known to last for up to four hours. After a nap, hunters resume their activities at dusk.

THE HUNTING PARTY

Some look forward to autumn as the traditional commencement of the hunting season. Whether one chooses to hunt or not, there are celebrations of this season to be had and traditions to be enjoyed.

When I think of hunting, I am reminded of the film *Gosford Park*, which is set in the 1930s. In it, a gathering of wealthy British meet at an English manor for a weekend hunting party and the centerpiece of the weekend ends up being anything but hunting. Food, drink, and socializing occupy the plot as much as the manor guests—after all, posh hunting gatherings are all about what happens when you're not hunting. As you can imagine, this is how Champagne often enters the scene. Naturally, a day spent hunting in the outdoors is best capped off by a hearty, gratifying meal. Assuming one eats what one shoots, such a meal could include a roast of the day's prize. A hunter's meal is often rich with vegetables, game, and flavor, and is in fact the ideal pairing for any of the refreshing Veuve Clicquot vintages. Veuve Clicquot has two chefs, Laurent Beuve and Christophe Pannetier, who work closely with the winemaking team to create dishes to perfectly match the house wines. Here they share three of their favorite hunter's recipes to pair with some of the rarer vintages of our Champagne.

A shooting lunch at Veuve Clicquot's Verzy mansion. The lobster, duck, and berry tart is accompanied here by Veuve Clicquot vintages from 1953, 1980, 1988, and La Grande Dame 1990—here in a Jeroboam.

LOBSTER SALAD WITH CITRUS DRESSING

INGREDIENTS (serves 4):

FOR THE LOBSTER

1 onion

1 carrot

½ orange

½ lemon

1 bouquet garni (bundle of fresh herb sprigs and bay leaves)

½ fresh ginger cut into thick coins

1 tablespoon whole black peppercorns

1 tablespoon coriander seeds

Salt

2 1-1¼ pound lobsters

FOR THE SALAD

1 tablespoon freshly squeezed lemon juice

1 tablespoon freshly squeezed orange juice

1 tablespoon balsamic vinegar

1 shallot, minced

1 teaspoon Dijon mustard

Salt and freshly ground black pepper to taste

3 tablespoons olive oil

3 tablespoons hazelnut oil

8 ounces mesclun mixed salad greens

Make the lobster: Bring 2 quarts water to a boil in a large pot. Add the onion, carrot, orange, lemon, bouquet garni, ginger, peppercorns, coriander, and salt to taste. Cook for 15 minutes. Add the lobsters, cover the pot, and bring to a simmer; cook for 10 minutes. Drain the lobsters and plunge into ice water to stop the cooking; discard the aromatics. Cut off the head and use scissors to separate the shell from the meat. Crack the claws and remove the meat, keeping it in large pieces if possible.

Make the salad: In a large bowl, whisk together the lemon and orange juices, vinegar, shallot, mustard, and salt and pepper. Whisk in the oils. Toss the greens with some of the dressing and mound them on 4 serving plates. Toss the lobster meat with some of the remaining dressing and arrange it on top of the salad (½ tail and 1 claw per serving). Drizzle with any remaining dressing and serve immediately.

Serve with Veuve Clicquot Vintage 2002.

Duck à la Verzy and a carafed Veuve Clicquot Vintage Rich 1996. Carafing sweet Champagnes is recommended to remove some of the effervescence, which better suits their sweetness.

DUCK À LA VERZY

INGREDIENTS (serves 6):
1 cup duck stock
1 stick natural licorice root
3 carrots (purple, white, and orange)
1 large rutabaga
1 parsnip
1 Jerusalem artichoke
4 ounces Chinese artichokes
6 boneless duck breast halves, skin side scored
2 shallots, chopped
Salt and freshly ground black pepper
3 tablespoons unsalted butter
Ground licorice

Preheat the oven to 350°F.

In a small saucepan, bring the stock and licorice root to a simmer. Cook until the stock is syrupy and reduced by half; discard the licorice root. Set aside and keep warm.

Peel the carrots, rutabaga, parsnip, and Jerusalem artichoke and cut into bite-size chunks. Scrub the Chinese artichokes and cut them into chunks. Set aside.

Season the duck with salt and pepper. In a large ovenproof skillet, cook the duck skin side down until well browned. Transfer to the oven and roast until medium-rare. Remove the duck to a carving board and cover loosely with aluminum foil to keep warm.

To the same skillet, add the carrots, rutabaga, parsnip, Jerusalem and Chinese artichokes. Cook over medium heat, stirring frequently, until tender but still firm. Stir in the shallots and season with salt and pepper.

Add the butter to the stock reduction and stir until melted.

Slice the duck breasts crosswise. On individual serving plates, pile the vegetables, drizzle with some of the reduction, and top with the duck. Drizzle with any remaining reduction and sprinkle with ground licorice.

MIXED BERRY TARTS

INGREDIENTS (serves 6):
1 sheet frozen puff pastry (6 to 8 ounces), thawed
1 scant cup almond flour
½ cup confectioners' sugar, plus more to serve
2 tablespoons unsalted butter, melted
1 large egg
10 ounces (about 2 cups) mixed berries (such as blueberries and red currants)

Preheat the oven to 350°F. Line a baking sheet with parchment paper.

Roll out the pastry to less than ¼ inch thick and prick it with a fork all over. Use a 4-inch round cutter to cut out 6 rounds and arrange them on the prepared baking sheet. Set aside.

In a large bowl, whisk together the almond flour and confectioners' sugar, then stir in the butter. Stir in the egg and mix well to make a smooth, homogenous batter. Generously spread the batter over the pastry rounds and bake for about 12 minutes. Let cool to room temperature, then top with the berries. Sprinkle with confectioners' sugar and serve.

Serve with a sweet Champagne, such as Veuve Clicquot Demi-Sec or Veuve Clicquot Vintage Rich 2002.

THE SEASON AT GOODWOOD

by the Earl of March & Kinrara

Goodwood, home to the Dukes of Richmond, has been an important part of what is known in England as "the Season" for more than two hundred years, beginning with the Goodwood's first horse race meeting in 1802, at what is widely regarded as the most beautiful racecourse in the world. Edward VII helped to establish the Goodwood July race meeting as the super-fashionable occasion it became, making it one of the most socially important moments of the year.

Indeed, it was Edward VII who was responsible for "dressing down" and making it the relaxed, quintessentially English experience that it is today. The story goes that one year for the races he discarded his black top hat, which went with his morning dress and was de rigueur in the period, and donned a white one instead. All the young blades sent their valets to London immediately to find similar headgear. Most were disappointed, but they were ready and prepared with their white toppers the following year. But the king, confounding them all, came in a white linen suit. Ever since, Goodwood has been about linen suits and Panama hats—much nicer and cooler than the morning dress still worn at Ascot. From then on, the monarch of the period has always been a guest at the July race week which, over the years, has become fondly known as "Glorious Goodwood"—in recognition of the outstanding racing, the stupendous views across the south of England's most beautiful countryside, and the usually gorgeous weather.

Goodwood, though, is famous for more than just horse racing. Motor racing, golf, flying, shooting, and cricket also play a big part in Goodwood's season, all of them started by enthusiastic members of the Richmond family over the last three hundred years. The first game of cricket was played at Goodwood in 1702 and the earliest existing written rules of cricket are in the Goodwood archive.

Motor racing has played an increasingly important role on the estate since the ninth Duke of Richmond and Gordon, affectionately known as Freddie March and a successful driver himself, founded the demanding and famous circuit in 1948. It quickly became not only the home of British motor sport but also one of the social highlights of the year until he closed it in 1966. It remained dormant until I embarked on a project to rebuild it in 1991. It took more than seven years to obtain the appropriate planning permissions from the local authority and, in the meantime, we started the Goodwood Festival of Speed in 1993, which quickly became the biggest car culture event in the world and now attracts a crowd of well over 175,000.

Once the circuit was rebuilt exactly as it was in the 1950s, the Goodwood Revival was launched in 1998. It has not only become the most competitive historic motor racing event in the world but also an extraordinary sporting occasion, as it is the only major sporting event to take place completely within period themes of the 1940s, 1950s, and 1960s—everyone comes wearing period clothes, driving the correct cars, and even carrying the right picnic hampers!

The Festival of Speed and the Goodwood Revival are unique in that despite having been created in the last twenty-five years, these events have found themselves a permanent place on the English social summer calendar—those special few months in the English summer known as "the Season."

The glamorous Goodwood Revival, the biggest motor racing circuit of the year, is referred to as a "magical step back in time." Staged entirely in the time capsule of the 1940s, 1950s, and 1960s—from the classic, non-modernized racetrack to vintage autos—Goodwood relives the glory days and their glorious ways. THIS PAGE: Fangio-era Formula Ones open the show.

The Veuve Clicquot Bentley, a 1961 S2 Continental "Flying Spur," one of twenty-two with left-hand drive, was originally ordered by automotive headlights manufacturer Max Lucas for his beach house in Le Touquet, while a matching Tudor Grey right-hand drive version was simultaneously ordered for his villa in Southampton. After having passed through the hands of French rock legend Nino Ferrer, the car was purchased in 1989 by Count Edouard de Nazelle, a descendant of Madame Clicquot's business partner and heir Edouard Werlé, and subsequently repainted in Clicquot colors. It is still functioning, perfectly maintained, and used at Veuve Clicquot Season events around the globe.

Champagne toasts an array of occasions: General de Gaulle at the liberation of Nazi-occupied Paris; more lightheartedly, period-dressed air hostesses at Goodwood Revival.

Veuve Clicquot's butler Abdel El Haddaoui
carries a tray of goodies at a picnic.

CHIC PICNIC

A successful picnic begins with the careful analysis of the possibilities at hand around you. Individual portions and cold foods are of the essence. Cutting is always complicated. Bring a large tablecloth and think of the occasion as any fancy or festive event: Do not hesitate to use real plates and silverware as well as sturdy glasses.

The pace of a typical picnic is somewhat different from that of any other meal. Cold cuts and raw vegetables (radishes, celery, carrots, and cauliflower, for example) make good appetizers while the grounds are tamed and the outdoor feast set out.

Assorted sandwiches should include everyone's favorites, but try limiting the main ingredients to two or three per sandwich: bacon, lettuce, and tomato; egg salad and watercress; turkey and brie.... Let your imagination be your guide, but make sure to include a wide variety of choices. Some family-style salads are always a good idea (a nice niçoise, for example), and potato and other vegetable chips are always a hit. Cheese and fruits make a pleasant, simple ending and can be nibbled on as the afternoon drags lazily and plans for all sorts of outdoor activities are devised. The Champagne of choice is Veuve Clicquot Yellow Label or Veuve Clicquot Rosé. Make sure to pack plenty of ice in the cooler.

Finally, besides food, think of what else might make a difference in your friends' comfort and enjoyment of the day: a first-aid kit, bug repellent, allergy medicine, a deck of cards, beach tennis rackets, some music....

Loading up the Bentley for a picnic, in the courtyard of the Manoir de Verzy.

YELLOWEEN

"Veuve Clicquot's Yelloween project is quite playful. It was amusing to create the ultimate carnival accessory, an evolution from one of my flagship bow ties, this time as a trompe l'oeil. Paper cut outs are reminiscent of an eighteenth-century masquerade ball, light and absolutely frivolous — the ideal accessory for a Halloween Champagne celebration."

—*Alexis Mabille*

Halloween with a Clicquot twist: Yelloween paints the world yellow with Veuve Clicquot events in thirty cities across the world. Few events are more festive at any time of the year, Yelloween bewitches with bubbly every October. THIS PAGE: Halloween illumination inside Veuve Clicquot's Reims mansion, Hôtel du Marc.

HALLOWEEN RECIPES

TRUFFLE PUMPKIN SOUP

INGREDIENTS (serves 4):
2¼ pounds peeled and seeded pumpkin (about 8½ cups), chopped
1 sweet onion, thinly sliced
3½ tablespoons unsalted butter
4 cups chicken broth
Salt and freshly ground black pepper
¾ cup sour cream
1 preserved truffle and its juice

Put the pumpkin in a large saucepan with the onion and half the butter. Add the broth and salt to taste, then bring to a simmer and cook for 10 minutes. Puree with an immersion blender (or in batches in a stand blender), adding the sour cream, the remaining butter, the truffle juice, and pepper to taste. Ladle into serving bowls and thinly slice the truffle over the soup. Serve.

NOTE: Truffle oil can give a kick to any truffle dish, but it is always made with synthetic aromas. It is basically truffle perfume. While it fools the nose with the idea of an abundant infusion of the precious mushroom, it is as shallow in the mouth as it is pungent. The characteristic long-lasting flavor of truffles can even be obliterated by the use of synthetic oil. Truffles are subtle, discreet, and shy.

Serve with Veuve Clicquot Vintage 1990 or 1993.

ROASTED CLEMENTINES WITH
RASPBERRY & BLACKBERRY COULIS

INGREDIENTS (serves 6):
12 clementines
1½ tablespoons unsalted butter
2 tablespoons maple syrup
1 glass clementine juice
6 tablespoons raspberry and blackberry coulis

Peel the clementines and slice off the white pith.

In a medium sauté pan, melt the butter and the syrup. When the butter is foaming, add the clementines and cook, turning occasionally, until blond and slightly crisp on the outside. Add the clementine juice. The outside should be candied and the flesh should be firm. Serve hot, drizzled with the coulis.

WINTER

WINTER

During winter in the Champagne region, the vines go into hibernation, awaiting the return of the spring sun. But for the winemaker, winter is a very busy season, as this is when the wine gets made.

In autumn, the grapes were picked, pressed, and separated into vats by vineyard and grape variety to undergo both a primary alcoholic and malolactic fermentation, the latter balancing out the acidity in the wine. Winter then becomes the occasion for reserve or current-year wine tastings. The wine will eventually be bottled with natural yeast and put into the cellar to age and transform into sparkling wine. But before this can happen, a perfectly balanced wine must be created by the art of blending.

WINTER BLENDING

Dominique Demarville

It is no exaggeration to call wine blending an art. The winemaker must be familiar with each of the flavors available to his palate, and there are thousands. He is expected to blend these flavors—as if on a canvas—into a bottle and produce a Champagne masterpiece, one that is consistent with past years' characteristics as well as with the house style. Veuve Clicquot has more than 1,300 acres (550 hectares) of vineyards and the average vat of wine is the product of one acre (½ hectare) of vineyard; this gives an idea of the sheer volume and variety of different wines we produce, all of which must be considered while blending.

I often compare winemaking to perfume making, as they are based on a similar concept: one uses many different sensorial experiences to create a single pleasurable blend. I believe that the ability to create these sensorial pleasures is an inherent talent. But there is a key difference between winemaking and perfume making: a winemaker's ingredients vary from year to year. Moreover, the winemaker must be able to imagine how his ingredients will blend and taste after three or more years of aging—not an easy prospect. This art form requires great skill as well as imagination.

At Veuve Clicquot we have an eight-person winemaking team that I head as cellar master. Due to the natural variations of the raw materials, the team must work hard to maintain the quality and style that Veuve Clicquot consistently delivers—year in and year out. I make the final decision as to which specific blends to use for our Champagnes, a complicated task that requires both an understanding of innumerable, subtle complexities and years of experience.

In 240 years there have been only ten cellar masters at Veuve Clicquot. The secrets of the trade—and passion for it—are passed down from master to master. I trained with Jacques Peters, the former cellar master, for three years before I was ready to assume my position at Veuve Clicquot. Such a transition period alone attests to the complicated nature of this trade and how gravely important the transmission process is, as well as the choice of successor.

The motto we adhere to at Veuve Clicquot was first stated by Madame Clicquot herself: "Only one quality: the finest." The cellar master who creates our Champagnes must apply this tenet to everything he does, guaranteeing consistent quality while continuing the tradition of his predecessors.

As many as one thousand different kinds of still wines can be used to elaborate Veuve Clicquot Yellow Label blend each year.

Tastings of the year's still wines takes up most of
the winter and spring months.

DOMINIQUE DEMARVILLE

Tenth Cellar Master at Veuve Clicquot

Champagne is called the "wine of the gods," in part due to the complexity of its elaboration, which is less a recipe than a form of alchemy.

Q: Why isn't there a year on the labels of most bottles of Champagne?
A: Champagne is typically a blend of wines from several harvests. Blending is of the essence in Champagne. Ever since 1772, we at Veuve Clicquot have developed specialized blending techniques that will produce a consistent wine year after year, a Champagne that bears the distinctive style of the House of Veuve Clicquot.
Q: How consistent is the quality of the wines of each year?
A: There are great years, such as 2006, 2004, and 1990, to speak of recent vintages. And lesser years, such as 2007 and 2003. During these latter years, we include a larger proportion of reserve wines in the base blend, so as to ensure the consistency of our signature Yellow Label.
Q: So the result is the same taste?
A: The "Clicquot style" includes variations around a common personality. Our wines are like members of a close family with similar characteristics. Moreover, a particularity of wine is that it ages. A Yellow Label blended in 1953 is going to be quite different from a wine blended more recently. But one can still tell they belong to the same family.
Q: What are the different grape varieties?
A: There are three kinds of grapes in Champagne: Chardonnay,

Pinot Meunier, and Pinot Noir. Veuve Clicquot is a blend of the three, with a larger proportion of the latter, which makes it a rather full-bodied Champagne.
Q: What are the other complexities of Champagne making?
A: Our vineyard is not in one block, like most modern-day wineries, but rather atomized in small fields scattered across the entire Champagne region. Each field is harvested and vinified separately. This gives us more than one thousand wines every year, which need to be tasted one by one and then assembled to produce the result we seek. And, of course, the trick is to imagine how the blend will taste after it ages—for a minimum of three years—in our cellars.
Q: So what makes Veuve Clicquot so representative of fine Champagne?
A: Veuve Clicquot has a strong and steady personality. Yet contrary to what one might think, what has ensured the consistency of our Champagne for more than 240 years is not one formulaic recipe to be repeated year after year. Rather, it is an alchemy that takes into account the variety of ingredients, the diversity of the climate and harvests, the richness of terroirs, and the complexity of grape categories—and which allows time to do the rest.

CHAMPAGNE AND TRUFFLE CHEESE FONDUE

INGREDIENTS (serves 4 to 6):
½ bottle Veuve Clicquot Yellow Label
8 ounces Swiss cheese, shredded
2 tablespoons Gruyère cheese, shredded
2 tablespoons all purpose flour
1 teaspoon freshly grated nutmeg
1 preserved truffle, chopped, and its juice
1 1-pound loaf French bread, cut into 1-inch cubes
Salt and freshly ground black pepper

In a fondue pot, simmer the Champagne. A handful at a time, add the cheeses, stirring until each addition is melted before adding the next. Stir in the flour, nutmeg, truffle, and truffle juice and season with salt. Serve with the bread and long fondue forks.

A popular game of polo in the snow.

Veuve Clicquot bottles chill in the snow at a Thredbo
Ski Resort Season celebration in Australia.

The hottest scene during the cold winter months is on the ski slopes, so naturally that is where the Veuve Clicquot Season events tend to be. Whether at a chalet lunch overlooking the slopes or an *après-ski* party after a last run, Champagne provides the sparkle and excitement of sun on fresh powder. At *après-ski* fetes and ice raw bars, Veuve Clicquot is the drink of ski fashion at resorts across Vail and Aspen.

RIO CARNAVAL

Winter means cold winds and snow, but only to the northern half of the world. The southern hemisphere actually anticipates our months of winter with glee—to them, these months mean the return of the sun and its warmth, bringing growth and rejuvenation. But luckily for those of us who live north of the equator, we can always toss aside winter blues and take a holiday in the sunny south.

Rio de Janeiro is the ultimate party in the sun. Every February brings Carnaval, the biggest holiday in Brazil, attracting 70 percent of the country's annual tourism for a weeklong festival. Elaborate Brazilian costumes, samba parades, and parties all day (and night) long make this a festival that is unparalleled in the world. The fun simply screams for Champagne celebration—and Veuve Clicquot is there.

Inspired by the delicious Brazil style, I asked some Brazilian bartender friends to create a cocktail worthy of the "sacrifice" of mixing Veuve Clicquot Yellow Label. I was not disappointed. Deciding to get in the game myself, I also share with you some Champagne cocktail creations à la Brésil.

CARNAVAL COCKTAILS

CAIPI-CLICQUOT

INGREDIENTS (makes 1)
Crushed ice
2 ounces cachaça
1 lime, cut into wedges
3 fresh lychees, peeled and pitted, crushed
2 ounces lychee syrup
Veuve Clicquot Yellow Label

Fill a shaker with crushed ice, add the cachaça, squeezed lime wedges, crushed lychees, and lychee syrup, and shake well. Pour into a large tumbler and top up with a splash of Champagne.

CLICQUOTROSKA

INGREDIENTS (makes 1)
Crushed ice
2 ounces vodka
8 ounces passion-fruit pulp
Veuve Clicquot Yellow Label

Fill a shaker with crushed ice, pour in the vodka and passion-fruit pulp, and shake well. Pour into a tall glass three quarters full and top up with Champagne. No added sugar needed.

CARNAVAL QUEEN

by Adriane Galisteu

Carnaval, as they call the festive season in Brazil, is not merely a popular celebration founded on the spirit of the Latin *carne vale*, which means "farewell to flesh." It is the greatest show on Earth. I am a lover of Carnaval, having participated in its events for sixteen years now, day and night. Nowhere is it better to be than in front of the drum orchestra section—the sound of the *cuíca*, the rhythm of the *tamborim*, the beat of the bass drum that moves our souls to the beat of a samba.

A samba school parade is much more than fancy dress and dancing. You have to leave behind everyday life and all of your troubles to let yourself go into a kind of trance—the gift of samba music that is sparked by the surrender of your soul and disciplined by technical precision. You and your samba school must rehearse extensively for this moment before the judges, who score the school's expertise and harmony in singing, dancing, acting, and engaging with and delighting the audience.

At Carnaval, we dance to honor the dedication of musicians who have worked hard all year, as well as whole communities that have embodied dreams in the elaborate floats, costumes, and choreography. We also dance for the passionate fans who cheer for their favorite samba schools. Carnaval is the most fun, the funniest, and yet most serious thing in the world.

Carnaval is also the most democratic party in the world; the poor might become kings, the rich might lose their power, and race, color, and size of bank account matter not at all. Everyone has the same goal: the title of champion samba school. Despite thunderstorms, searing heat, heavy costumes, and unforgiving stopwatches, we dancers and players balance on vertiginous high heels, both to make history and give our best. After all, there is no party that best reflects the Brazilian people's happy-go-lucky, passionate, and competitive nature than Carnaval.

But if the greatest poets in the world cannot describe Carnaval, who am I to try? My feeling for it is beyond any definition or explanation; I simply love it.

Drum queen of Unidos da Tijuca and Brazil's sweetheart, Adriane Galisteu awaits the results of the 2011 Rio carnival.

Formal carnival celebration in the
Opera House, Rio de Janeiro.

Dancers at the Rio carnival.

TRUFFLE SEASON

Champagne and Christmas are happiness and decadence intertwined. The Christmas season means time to enjoy what you eat, while eating what you enjoy! Although Champagne pairs with virtually any holiday delicacy or celebration, it is unforgettably divine with truffles. As truffle season runs from around mid-December to the end of February, to me Christmastime means truffles and Veuve Clicquot.

Truffles often retain a bit of a mystery, as they are considered by most a rarity and a delicacy. But to me, they are a common sight: I grew up in the southwest part of France, a region in which black truffles grow wild. And though truffles were a familiar part of my entire childhood, no truffle was ever wasted!

Hunting for wild truffles was always a highly anticipated event. I still enjoy searching for them when I go home each winter. Truffles are hidden underground, so they are best found with a trained dog or pig, as these animals have a natural ability as well as a penchant to seek out the tasty underground treats.

Truffles, or *Tuber melanosporum* by their Latin name, are referred to as "black diamonds" not only because they are rare and fetch a high price at market, but also because of their delectable, rich flavor. Truffles tend to grow under and around the roots of old oak trees, and the largest truffle market in southwest France is at Lalbenque in Quercy, near my family home. Lalbenque is known by chefs worldwide and is at its busiest in January, when black truffles emit their most intense perfume.

Growing up around truffles meant that I got to sample a lot of them too; home cooking often meant truffle cooking. Of course the local cuisine from my region specializes in truffle recipes—even the idea makes me nostalgic for home! Since truffles are also a staple I use in my kitchen, I share with you one of my own secret recipes, a favorite that is sure to make you nostalgic too.

TRUFFLE RISOTTO

Through trial and error I have developed the perfect truffle risotto, sure to melt in your mouth. Before you begin to make it, plan your week accordingly: I recommend you pick your truffles on a Sunday and cook the risotto on a Tuesday. Between Sunday and Tuesday, let the truffles sit with the uncooked risotto rice—this will infuse it with even more flavor.

INGREDIENTS (serves 8)
3 tablespoons of olive oil
1 packet riso carnaroli (Italian short-grain risotto rice)
Chicken and/or beef stock (best if you have both, but chicken preferable)
1/3 bottle Veuve Clicquot Yellow Label Champagne
1 to 2 cups of panna da cucina (thick Italian cream), to taste
1 cup Parmesan cheese shavings
Truffle peels (crumbled), to taste
Truffles (pre-peeled and very thinly sliced), to taste

Heat a few tablespoons of olive oil in a large pot on a stove at medium-high heat. Once oil is hot, add rice and stir until rice takes on a transparent appearance. Douse rice with 1/3 bottle of Veuve Clicquot; continue stirring as it cooks down. Add stock to the rice as it absorbs it, slowly, a splash at a time. Stir constantly: do not allow the rice to stick to the pot. Cook and stir about 10 minutes. Just before you turn down the heat, add panna and stir through. Turn heat to very low. Add Parmesan shavings and stir. Add crumbled truffle peels for texture, and stir. Turn off heat. Add a healthy pat of butter to "make it shine." Stir and serve into soup plates. Just before serving to your guests, add at least half of a shaved truffle on top of each of the plates—don't skimp.

Note: This recipe will also reheat beautifully. If (somehow) there is some risotto remaining, it will taste equally as scrumptious the next day, if not better, than the day it was made. Add some stock and reheat, enjoy again!

CHAMPAGNE CHRISTMAS

by Chez l'Ami Louis

POMMES FRITES

The secret to the perfect French fries is frying them twice, once to precook and again just before serving. Be very careful to watch the temperature of the oil: If it is not hot enough, your fries will be soggy; if it is too hot, they'll burn and become bitter.

INGREDIENTS (serves 6):
2¼ pounds Bintje potatoes
Vegetable oil for deep-frying
Salt to taste

Peel, rinse, and cut the potatoes to the size you like, from thick fingers to matchsticks (allumettes).

Heat the oil in a deep, heavy pot. When the oil is hot enough, carefully add about one-third of the potatoes and stir gently so they don't stick to one another. As they rise to the surface, remove them with a wire skimmer or slotted spoon and let drain on paper towels. Repeat with the remaining potatoes.

When ready to serve, fry the potatoes again, one small portion at a time, just until nicely browned. Drain on fresh paper towels. Add salt to the hot fries and repeat with the remaining potatoes.

The famed bistro L'Ami Louis in the Marais area of Paris.

FOIE GRAS

Making one's own foie gras is a lengthy and fastidious process that is not recommended to the layman. However, in what is commonly referred to as pâté in English, there is a vast selection of ready-made products available. Here are a few tips for purchasing pâté: First of all, pick your animal, goose or duck. Goose foie gras is very subtle in taste and has a creamier and smoother texture. It is generally a bit pricier and can be flavored with Armagnac. It is considered by some to be a bit less digestible than its duck counterpart.

Duck foie gras has a slightly more robust taste and texture and is easier to find and favored by most over goose. It can be bought fresh, to panfry or make your own terrine. A favorite is the *mi-cuit*, or "half-cooked" foie gras, which has been partly cooked in broth and is available vacuum-packed. It has a short shelf life. If you opt for the preserved version, a glass container usually guarantees *foie gras entier*—that is, whole foie gras, which does not mean that one gets the whole liver, but that no other ingredients have been added. *Bloc de foie gras* varies from excellent to doubtful; avoid foie gras "mousse," as it is made of pork and flavored with duck.

EASY DUCK CONFIT

Potted duck or duck confit, usually bought prepared, is the meat of the fatty duck that is used to make foie gras. As foie gras is extracted and prepared, the meat of the duck is slow-cooked in its own fat. It is put in a glass jar or canned and covered with the fat, which preserves it. This method will give a crispier and slightly less greasy version than the traditional panfried method. Serve with potato sarladaise or simple potatoes roasted with the duck fat.

(serves 4):

Preheat the oven to 450°F.

Open a 16- to 20-ounce glass jar or can of duck confit, available online or at gourmet specialty shops, and extract the pieces of duck from the fat. Remove as much fat as possible by gently scraping it with a wooden spatula. Finish sponging it with a paper towel.

In a heavy skillet, panfry the meat side until browned. Transfer to a rack set over a rimmed baking sheet and bake for 10 to 15 minutes, until crisp. Serve.

ESCARGOTS

INGREDIENTS (serves 6):
1 cup (2 sticks) unsalted butter, slightly softened
¼ cup finely chopped fresh parsley
2 shallots, finely chopped
1 clove garlic, finely chopped
36 frozen or canned French snails
36 snail shells

Preheat the oven to 350°F.

In a medium bowl, combine the butter, parsley, shallots, and garlic. Place a snail in each shell and fill the cavity with the butter mixture. Arrange on a rimmed baking sheet and bake for 10 to 12 minutes. Serve hot in individual snail dishes, with snail tongs and forks.

———

THE BEST ROAST CHICKEN IN THE WORLD

INGREDIENTS (serves 4):
1 whole chicken, giblets removed from the cavity
1 bunch fresh thyme, plus some thyme flowers for garnish
7 tablespoons unsalted butter, at room temperature
Salt and freshly ground black pepper

Preheat the oven to 375°F.

Stuff the chicken with the entire bunch of thyme. Smear the chicken with a generous layer of butter. Put the chicken in an oval ceramic baking dish, breast side up, and roast for 1 hour, regularly spreading the melted butter and juices over the chicken, until nicely browned and crisp on the top. If you like, turn the chicken upside down and roast until the bottom is crispy.

Remove from the oven and season with salt and pepper. Sprinkle with a few thyme flowers. Collect the sauce from the bottom of the pan and serve it in a gravy boat alongside the chicken.

Serve with Veuve Clicquot Rosé 1985 or Veuve Clicquot 1990.

ETON MESS WITH WILD STRAWBERRIES

INGREDIENTS (serves 4):
4 cups whipped cream
4 to 6 ounces meringue
1 quart wild strawberries, rinsed and hulled
Vanilla sugar (optional)

Put half the whipped cream in a large bowl. Crush the meringue and gently fold it into half the whipped cream. On serving plates, pile meringue cream on one side and plain cream on the other. Top with the strawberries and sprinkle with vanilla sugar if desired. Serve.

SPRING

SPRING

Spring sings of excitement and new beginnings. When I am standing in the fields of Champagne, I feel anticipation in the air. New life, buds, vines, wine— and yes, like tender green buds poking out of formerly barren branches, new Season parties also sprout up after months of hibernation.

SPRING IN THE CELLAR

Spring announces the impending peak of the Season. It is the excitement before the party, the buds before the grapes. As new vine shoots are just pushing out of the soil, the winemakers become very busy underground. The bottles that have been aging in the cellar for three, five, or seven years are ready for the next step of their complex journey to becoming Champagne—a process called disgorging. Using the riddling method that was invented by Madame Clicquot herself (and is now used in almost every Champagne house), the winemakers remove the sediment that has settled into the necks of the bottles that had been at rest, hibernating, you could say, upside down and at an angle. After a dosing liqueur is added, which will determine the relative sweetness or dryness of the wine from demi-sec to brut, the bottles are corked and laid in the cellars for the next few months. Then they are labeled and ready for consumption—and when it is time to pop the cork, remember to toast to spring!

After disgorgement, which removes the natural sediment, the bottles are topped off with a sweet mixture of still wine, which determines their sugar level—currently around 7 grams per liter for a Brut Champagne.

The traditional method of corking a bottle is no longer used, as the rope proved to grow fragile over time (and thus led to the unwanted explosion of too many precious bottles).

The Crayères are ancient Roman chalk mines in Reims, approximately one hundred feet underground. With constant humidity levels around 85 percent and a temperature of 50 to 55°F throughout the year, they offer perfect, natural, and energy-saving aging conditions. The fifteen miles of tunnels were bought by Madame Clicquot in the nineteenth century and host each bottle of Veuve Clicquot for a minimum of three years before it is released.

VEUVE CLICQUOT CELEBRATES DESIGN

Over time, the Veuve Clicquot House has come to epitomize distinctive design. The House's long history of innovation has made it a natural leader in the design field, both in collaborations and inventions. It was, in fact, Madame Clicquot herself who began the avant-garde culture that is today the trademark of Veuve Clicquot.

In constantly exploring new territories and how best to build her business, Madame Clicquot was a woman of determination and foresight. In 1816 she invented the riddling table (*la table de remuage*), which allowed sediment to collect in the necks of bottles for easier expulsion, producing wines that were clear, as we have today. She was a firm believer that Champagne should be clear to be properly enjoyed and of the utmost quality.

Madame Clicquot's invention was historic, and the process of riddling is still used today. The riddling table, with its aesthetic as well as functional value, also qualifies as the company's first act of industrial design; this groundbreaking invention combined science and art and indisputably improved production. Veuve Clicquot is proud of its namesake and her ingenious contributions to history and design. This led to collaborations with famed designers and studios such as Porsche, Tom Dixon, Mathieu Lehanneur–featured in the following pages.

Madame Clicquot's innovation not only is an iconic example of creativity in the Champagne industry, it has also proved a unique source of design inspiration. In 2005, the designer Andrée Putman created a reinterpretation of the riddling table to celebrate its two hundredth anniversary. Putman enthusiastically seized upon Madame Clicquot's ingenious yet simple concept, and her reinterpretation incorporated the charming yet unrealistic idea "that you could enjoy a chilled bottle directly on the riddling table." Andrée Putman transformed what was once a rustic innovation into a romantic contemporary table, evocative of the different stages of a procedure imagined two centuries earlier. She paired the table with two armchairs, a cozy table designed for a wine tasting *à deux*.

Vertical Limit, a Porsche-designed wine cooler hosting magnums of Veuve Clicquot's most prized vintages, from 1955 to 2002.

1962

1975

To celebrate the bicentennial of the Great Comet that crossed the skies of Champagne in 1811 and was rumored to have prompted the best-ever harvest at Veuve Clicquot, internationally acclaimed British designer Tom Dixon created the Comet Lamp. Here is a grouping of nearly one hundred of the lamps, as presented at the Milan Design Week.

DESIGN IN MILANO

To the Italians, springtime means design time. Milan Design Week, or the Salone Internazionale del Mobile, is the largest decoration trade fair in the world. Showcasing the very latest in design and furniture for the home, designers from around the world descend on the Italian financial capital to salivate over the most cutting-edge developments. More than two thousand companies exhibit at the event, setting up camp in the Milan Fairgrounds, which has an exhibition space of more than two million square feet (220,000 square meters).

Hundreds of thousands of people flock annually to Milan Design Week to catch a glimpse of the most state-of-the-art designs for the home. The population of the city grows by at least 25 percent during this time, and everything Milanese turns its gaze toward design.

In Paris, Fashion Week comes and goes and the average Parisian may not even be aware of its presence. Not so in Milan. Each neighborhood becomes a design mecca—and Veuve Clicquot is everywhere. Any festive event or party of the Champagne-worthy scene is dotted with flutes of Veuve Clicquot.

Design Week features the innovations of up-and-coming young designers. Of course, a star attraction at the festival is the Veuve Clicquot space, with unique commissioned pieces that define the cutting edge. Veuve Clicquot's commitment to creativity has led it to collaborate with some of the most talented names in the world of design, including Tom Dixon, 5.5 designers, Front Design, Mathieu Lehanneur, Christophe Pillet, Karim Rashid, Pablo Reinoso, and Porsche Design.

For Design Week 2010, Veuve Clicquot collaborated with Humberto and Fernando Campana to create a contemporary gloriette, a reinterpretation of the nineteenth-century gazebo. This modern reincarnation of a centuries-old garden was meant to provide a memorable venue for open-air Champagne tasting. The gloriette was designed for permanent residence in the garden of Veuve Clicquot's Hotel du Marc.

Once Upon a Dream, by Mathieu Lehanneur, a sleep capsule as well as an allegory around the mandatory three years of cellar aging of Veuve Clicquot's Yellow Label—considerably more than the eighteen months practiced by most houses in Champagne.

This loveseat, by Karim Rashid, reinterprets the classic eighteenth-century conversation seat.

DESIGN CULINAIRE

---

by Germain Bourré & Maryan Gandon, Hotel Fairmont, Monte Carlo

AIRY MILLE–FEUILLES

The strata of each of these creations were imagined to pay tribute to the different layers of aromas experienced in Veuve Clicquot's vintages.

Crabmeat on toasted white bread: 1 ounce cooked crabmeat, 2 tablespoons minced Granny Smith apple, 2 tablespoons minced mango

Ratatouille and red mullet on toasted white bread: 1½ ounces cooked red mullet fillets, ⅓ cup sautéed ratatouille (with fennel, baby zucchini, red bell peppers, eggplant, fresh thyme)

Smoked salmon on toasted whole-wheat bread: 2 ounces smoked salmon, 2 tablespoons crème fraîche or cream cheese with chives

Vegetables cooked in Carta Fata transparent cooking film on toasted white bread: baby carrots, fava beans, zucchini, asparagus, bell peppers, tomatoes

Sea bass tartare on toasted whole-wheat bread: 1½ ounces cooked sea bass fillet, 1 cup diced tomatoes

Serve with Veuve Clicquot Vintage 2002.

Each year culinary designer Germain Bourré develops a full-scale collaboration between France's most prestigious chefs and Maison Veuve Clicquot.

TERRESTRIAL FLIGHT

The subtle combinations of flavors and temperatures in the four elements of this selection
of dishes were designed to echo the nuanced aromas in the Veuve Clicquot Vintage Rosé.

Veal medallion with black-olive caviar on socca bread
Zucchini flower tempura
Tomatoes and Jabugo ham (jamón ibérico)
Mashed green peas with demi-sel butter

Serve with Veuve Clicquot Vintage Rosé 2004.

VEUVE CLICQUOT SOIRÉE

D Î N E R
au Palais de l'Élysée

en l'honneur

DES CHEFS DES GOUVERNEMENTS
DES PAYS MEMBRES DE L'O.T.A.N.

17 décembre 1957

Consommé aux pailles d'or

Suprêmes de soles Cardinal

Faisan rôti Châtelaine

Foie gras des Landes aux raisins

Salade Tourangelle

Parfait glacé Chanzy

Petits fours

Riesling (Grande Réserve) 1953
Château Haut-Brion 1937
La Tache (Domaine Romanée Conti) 1953
Veuve Clicquot 1949 en magnum

State Dinner at the Elysée Presidential Palace
In Honor of the Heads of State of NATO Members

17 December 1957

Gold Leaf Consommé
Roasted Pheasant "Châtelaine"
Foie Gras and Grapes
Goat Cheese Salad
Chocolate Ice Cream Cake
Petits Fours

Riesling (Grande Réserve) 1953
Château Haut-Brion 1937
La Tache (Domaine Romanée Conti) 1953
Veuve Clicquot 1949, served in magnums

It's French, It's Imported,

It's Clicquot CHAMPAGNE

PROMINENTLY SERVED SINCE 1772 • VEUVE CLICQUOT-PONSARDIN REIMS, FRANCE
SOLE DISTRIBUTORS FOR THE U.S.A. THE JOS. GARNEAU CO., NEW YORK CITY

Veuve Clicquot's *soirée entre amis* in the gardens of the Musée Nissim de Camondo, Paris, on June 15, 2010.

A popular traditional game originated in the south of France, *pétanque* has its cosmopolitan chic version with Veuve Clicquot. In couture and high heels, British socialite Rebecca Mitchell Carcelle, San Diego sweetheart Lucy Little, and Russian designer Liana Yaroslavsky.

SUMMER

Poolside at Rio de Janeiro's Hotel Santa Teresa.

SUMMER

Summer. Just the word itself conjures ephemeral joys: basking in the sun, splashing in the pool, feeling sand under your feet, enjoying fresh seafood and Champagne in the out-of-doors. Summer evokes a sentiment both blissfully positive and entirely relaxing.

SUMMER IN THE VINEYARD

One's professional life may pause during the summer months while social life comes into full swing. The days of summer, always fleeting are best spent outside—yachting, picnicking, watching polo, or sailing the seven seas. In summer, Veuve Clicquot Season events are almost exclusively held in the out-of-doors: the sun is hot, and the scene even hotter.

Whether sun-kissed skin or sandals, the season's styles lead to a stylish Season. Summer events provide the ultimate venues to see and to be seen at your most beautiful. Every Season event calls for a different mode of fashion, be it the strappy sundress or the white linen suit, the huge hat for the polo match or the sunglasses for the yacht. And it goes without saying: a Season attendee must also accessorize with a Champagne glass in hand.

While we soak up the summer sun, Champagne vines do the same. In the Champagne region, summer is a crucial time. Even though this season is the least busy time for working in the field, it is the most important time for the field. It is when each vintage is put to the test.

Champagne is farther north than other wine regions, so it is somewhat cooler and has a more variable rainfall. Our region's wine production especially lies in the hands of the weather gods: With too much rain, the wine can be of a lesser quality and more diluted. With too little, the grapes will not properly mature. August is the month of truth—a sunny August is necessary for the perfect grape maturation.

To the hardworking Champagne maker, this climactic month is rather thrilling. At its end we celebrate the end of the Champagne cycle—with some Champagne, of course.

A yellow saddle designed by British designer Nigel Coates is the reward for the winning team of the much-acclaimed Veuve Clicquot Gold Cup Polo finals in Cowdray Park, West Sussex, United Kingdom

SUMMER SOCIAL SPORTS

To spy the latest summer styles, there are few places better than at a polo match. From Cowdray Park in West Sussex to Governors Island in New York City, Veuve Clicquot is polo's partner across the world. Veuve Clicquot's comprehensive polo program pairs the "sport of kings" with the drink of decadence, and today the two are absolutely inseparable.

Come every June, the Veuve Clicquot Polo Classic returns to Governors Island, in the heart of New York City, to feature glamorous guests and the thrill of polo.

Amid a sea of signature Yellow Label umbrellas, Veuve Clicquot is served to a convivial crowd of celebrities and aficionados alike.

At this American occasion comparable only to a royal European wedding, Polo Classic spectators boast the Season's most fashionable looks and trends for the year to come. Enjoying spectacular views of the Manhattan skyline, the see-and-be-seens enjoy a polo match of world-class players, including event co-chair Nacho Figueras, captain of the Black Watch team.

His Royal Highness Prince Henry of Wales and Nacho Figueras at the third annual Veuve Clicquot Polo Classic on Governors Island, Manhattan, New York, in June 2010.

VEUVE CLICQUOT POLO

by Nacho Figueras

In 25 de Mayo, Argentina, where I grew up, polo is every gentleman's passion. It was natural for me to love this very ancient sport, and it became my mission to reintroduce it to New York City. Thanks to the fantastic collaboration with Veuve Clicquot, we are able, year after year, to provide a great afternoon of Champagne and polo to 18,000 New Yorkers.

Doing the same on the West Coast was the logical next step, and in 2010 we proudly brought high-goal polo to Will Rogers State Park in Pacific Palisades, Los Angeles.

It is an honor to be promoting such a classic sport all around the world with such an iconic brand as Veuve Clicquot.

Polo superstar Nacho Figueras kicks off the
Veuve Clicquot Polo Classic on Governors
Island, Manhattan, New York.

FOIE GRAS MOUSSE & SMOKED EEL

INGREDIENTS (serves 6):
5 ounces soft foie gras pâté
¾ cup sour cream
Salt and freshly ground black pepper
¾ teaspoon unflavored gelatin, dissolved in 1 tablespoon water
2 slices farmhouse bread
1 ounce smoked eel
2 tablespoons onion marmalade
Balsamic vinegar
6 mini bunches of fresh red currants

In a food processor, puree the foie gras. In a small bowl, whisk the sour cream and season with salt and pepper. Slowly melt the gelatin in a small saucepan over low heat, stirring. Gently fold the gelatin and the sour cream mixture into the foie gras.

From the bread, cut circles the size of the small serving glasses and toast them. Fit a toast circle into each glass. Separate the eel's sections and layer it over the toasts, alternating with the foie gras mixture and marmalade and finishing with the foie gras. Sprinkle balsamic vinegar over each serving and decorate each with a mini bunch of currants. Serve.

SMOKED SALMON TIRAMISU, SUN-DRIED TOMATOES, & PARMESAN CHEESE

INGREDIENTS (serves 6):
5 ounces smoked salmon
2 slices whole-wheat bread
Olive oil
Balsamic vinegar
1 cup mascarpone cheese
2 large eggs, separated
Mild red chili powder or paprika
8 sun-dried tomatoes
Handful of fresh arugula leaves
2 ounces Parmesan cheese

Dice the salmon. Toast the bread and sprinkle generously with oil and vinegar. From the toast, cut circles the size of the small serving glasses.

In a small bowl, whip the mascarpone and egg yolks until fluffy. Season with chili powder to taste. In a separate bowl, beat the egg whites until firm peaks form. Gently fold the whites into the mascarpone mixture. Layer the bread, salmon, mascarpone mixture, and tomatoes in the glass. Chill in the refrigerator for at least 2 hours. Garnish with grated Parmesan cheese, arugula leaves, and chili powder and serve.

A buffet set before a vertical garden designed by Veuve Clicquot's Véronique Boonefaes, for the annual Veuve Clicquot Business Woman Award Forum, featuring double magnums of La Grande Dame 1990 in both Brut and Rosé.

RASPBERRY MACARONS

INGREDIENTS (serves 12)

For the macarons:
1¾ cups (6 ounces) almond meal
1½ cups confectioners' sugar
3 large egg whites
¾ teaspoon salt
3 tablespoons granulated sugar
Red or pink food coloring

For the filling:
¼ cup egg whites (from about 2 large eggs), at room temperature
6 tablespoons granulated sugar
¼ teaspoon salt
10 tablespoons unsalted butter, cut into 1-inch pieces, at room temperature
3 tablespoons seedless raspberry jam, plus 3 teaspoons raspberry jam with seeds
1 cup fresh raspberries

FOR THE MACAROONS: Line two baking sheets with parchment paper. In a medium bowl, combine the almond meal and confectioners' sugar. In a separate large bowl, beat the egg whites together with the salt until foamy, then gradually add the granulated sugar, beating until stiff peaks form. Add drops of food coloring to reach desired shade. Fold in the almond mixture with a rubber spatula until completely incorporated. Spoon the batter into a pastry bag fitted with a plain tip and pipe peaked mounds onto the prepared baking sheets about 1½ inches apart. Let stand at room temperature until the tops are no longer sticky and a light crust forms, 20 to 30 minutes.

Preheat the oven to 300°F and position the racks in the upper and lower thirds of the oven and bake the macarons until crisp, 20 to 25 minutes. Transfer the baking sheets to wire racks and let cool completely, about 30 minutes.

FOR THE FILLING: In the bowl of a heavy-duty stand mixer, combine the egg whites, the 6 tablespoons sugar, and the salt. Set the bowl over a saucepan of simmering water and heat, stirring often, until the mixture registers 140°F on a candy thermometer, 3 to 4 minutes. Transfer the bowl to the mixer fitted with the whisk attachment and beat on high speed until stiff peaks form and the mixture has cooled to room temperature, 5 to 6 minutes. With the mixer running, add the butter, one piece at a time, beating until each piece is incorporated before adding the next. Add the seedless jam, 1 tablespoon at a time, beating to blend well after each addition.

Using ½ teaspoon jam with seeds for each, spread jam over flat side of half of the macarons. Spoon the buttercream into a pastry bag fitted with a ¼-inch plain tip. Starting at the outer edge of the flat sides of the remaining macarons, pipe the buttercream over in a spiral. Add a fresh raspberry in the middle. Gently press macarons, jam filled side down, onto buttercream coated macarons. Serve.

Preparations for the 2010 Le Fooding New York
food festival at MoMA PS 1 Contemporary Art
Center in Queens, New York.

The dashboard of a coveted vintage Riva yatch.

RIVA YACHTING

by Lia Riva

It could only be destiny, the king of the Riviera meeting the star of the Grand Crus of Champagne. And from this fateful confluence of two brands sharing a passion for excellence, a collaboration ensued. With luxury Italian motor yacht maker Riva, Veuve Clicquot has produced a La Grande Dame Cruise Collection of coolers and accessories for discerning yachtsmen.

Riva yachts and Veuve Clicquot Champagne both resonate with sophistication. Quality materials and craftsmanship have made Riva the most esteemed name in the world of yachting—its yachts were already legendary during the golden age of the Riviera and are now collected by twenty-first-century aficionados. As the company motto says, "To own a Riva is to be part of a dream...."

Generations of talent have gone into fashioning the sleekest of boats; years of skill have gone into blending the finest of Champagnes, both to the appreciation of connoisseurs worldwide. La Grande Dame by Riva, with its sleek and luxurious accents, epitomizes a philosophy and an art of living like none other.

The Cruise Collection, a wet bar created for a Riva
yacht owner by Veuve Clicquot in 2008.

"Extraordinary personalities with unique destinies, Pietro Riva and Barbe-Nicole Clicquot Ponsardin were legends in the luxury industry, each revolutionizing his or her respective domains in a brief span of time. They missed knowing each other by only a handful of years...ironic, as now both Riva and Veuve Clicquot portray the perfect combination of tradition and innovation, glamour and sophistication."

—Lia Riva

CLICQUOT ON THE BEACH

Poolside, seaside, or simply wherever the sun is, there is no better refreshment than a chilled glass of Champagne, and Veuve Clicquot has become the choice to fête any summer Season event. Clicquot innovation has developed its own funky accessories to keep its reinvigorating Champagne cool.

In France, one of the traditional summer pastimes is the game of *pétanque*. *Pétanque* is a versatile outdoor game that can be played on any occasion where there are willing and spirited partygoers. One needs limited skill and a bit of luck, but when coupled with Champagne, the game promises a chic afternoon of fun. Veuve Clicquot has a long tradition with the game and hosts annual block parties with pétanque courts in celebration of France's Bastille Day, every July 14.

A fire pit on the beach with waves lapping on the sand, the catch of the day roasting on the hot coals while the sun sets into the ocean: this scene calls for a chilled glass of Veuve Clicquot Rosé Champagne, reminiscent of the color of the fiery sky.

Whether in Rio or Miami, Phuket or Saint-Tropez, there are few other ingredients needed to add to this delicious recipe: good companionship, beach games, singing. Feel free to make plans as the evening unfolds but no worries: You have all the time in the world—the ultimate luxury.

EAT YOUR VEGGIES LE CLUB 55 STYLE

Saint Tropez

There isn't a better place to summer than Saint-Tropez. Smack-dab in the heart of the gorgeous French Riviera and teeming with celebrities, Saint-Tropez is the summer scene. Formerly a sleepy fishing town, Saint-Tropez was the central residence of the infamous Brigitte Bardot, who is often credited for putting the town on the map. The Saint-Tropez of today has been dubbed the playground of jet-setters, fashion models, and millionaires, and it boasts idyllic weather, pristine beaches, and an unreal nightlife. To top it off, the local cuisine is divine.

A favorite beachside restaurant is the notorious Le Club 55. A hot day at the beach is perfectly complemented by the restaurant's fresh fare. One of the most famous starters is the *panier de crudités* served with anchovy butter—light, scrumptious, and decadently paired with a glass of Veuve Clicquot.

RAW BASKET AT CLUB 55

INGREDIENTS (serves 6):
6 tomatoes
1 bunch baby artichokes
1 bunch scallions or spring onions
1 bunch radishes
1 bunch young carrots
1 bunch celery
1 fennel bulb
1 red bell pepper
1 cucumber
1 lemon
2 ounces white button mushrooms
6 hard-boiled eggs
Anchovy-black pepper mayonaise

The most difficult thing may be to source the raw cork dish in which the raw vegetables basket is best presented. Alternatively, a folky basket can be used.

A raw basket in good company at the legendary Saint-Tropez beach hangout Le Club 55, named after the year the restaurant started on a quid pro quo basis, catering to Brigitte Bardot and the cast of Roger Vadim's *And God Created Woman*.

POOLSIDE RECIPES

by Damien Montecer, executive chef at Hotel Santa Teresa, Rio de Janeiro

SALMON TARTARE

INGREDIENTS (serves 4):
8 ounces fresh boneless salmon, diced
1 jalapeño pepper, seeded and minced
1 tablespoon grated fresh ginger
1 tablespoon chopped fresh cilantro
1 tablespoon chopped fresh dill
1 teaspoon sesame oil
1 tablespoon mayonnaise

In a medium bowl, combine all the ingredients. Refrigerate until very cold before serving.

PLANTAIN SPRING ROLLS

INGREDIENTS (serves 4):
2 yellow plantains, peeled and finely diced
1 red bell pepper, finely diced
1 tablespoon grated fresh ginger
1 teaspoon chopped fresh cilantro
1 teaspoon chopped fresh dill
1 teaspoon sesame oil
Salt, to taste
4 rice paper wrappers

In a medium bowl, combine all the ingredients except the rice paper wrappers. Soften the wrappers one at a time in hot water, then divide the filling among them, folding the ends in and rolling them up tightly. Refrigerate until very cold before serving.

Jumbo shrimp grilling in Búzios' Insólito hotel fire pit.

TIGER SHRIMP TEMPURA

INGREDIENTS (serves 4):
2 cups all-purpose flour, plus more for dredging
1 cup cornstarch
4 teaspoons baking powder
1¾ cups ice water
Vegetable oil for deep-frying
8 to 10 large shrimp, peeled and deveined
Lime wedges
Coarse sea salt, crushed

In a medium bowl, whisk the flour, cornstarch, baking powder, and ice water together until fluffy.

Heat 2 inches of oil in a heavy pot until a bit of the batter sizzles when dropped into the oil. Dredge the shrimp in flour, dip in the batter, then carefully slide them into the hot oil. Fry until browned and cooked through. Drain on paper towels. Serve hot with lime wedges and salt.

TARTARE SAUCE

INGREDIENTS:
¾ cup mayonnaise
¾ cup chopped capers
¾ chopped gherkins
Juice of 1 lemon
¼ cup chopped fresh parsley
¼ cup chopped fresh dill
Salt and freshly ground black pepper

In a medium bowl, combine all the ingredients. Refrigerate until very cold before serving.

A hot-air balloon looms over a night golf game
in Spain.

ACKNOWLEDGMENTS

The author would like to thank Charles Miers, publisher of Rizzoli International Publications, and editor Dung Ngo.

Thanks also to Christophe Navarre, president of Moët Hennessy; Gilles Hennessy; Stéphane Baschiera, president of Veuve Clicquot; and Sabina Belli, and Antoine Cohen-Potin, for their constant support of this project.

Special thanks to the contributors of this book: Sir Elton John and David Furnish, Lord Charles March, Alexis Mabille, Adriane Galisteu, Alexandre Iodice, Nacho Figueras, Lia Riva Ferrarese, and Dominique Demarville, Tenth Cellar Master of Veuve Clicquot.

Thanks to these chefs and restaurant owners who have allowed me to poach their brilliant recipes: Patrice de Colmont (Le Club 55, Ramatuelle); Chef, Juan and Aymeric (Hotel Santa Teresa, Rio de Janeiro); Emmanuelle de Clermont-Tonnerre and Philippe Meeus (Insólito, Búzios); Louis and Chef Bibi (L'Ami Louis, Paris); Kiko (Kai, Paris); and, of course, Veuve Clicquot's excellent Laurent Beuve and Christophe Pannetier.

Thanks to all to whom we owe this visual depiction of the Season: Stéphane Feugère, Georgia Glynn Smith, Max von Gumppenberg, Xavier Lavictoire, Régine Mahaux, and Thibaut de Saint Chamas.

Thanks to Veuve Clicquot's favorite designers, as featured in order of appearance in this book: Christian Schwamkrug at Porsche Design Studio, Tom Dixon, Karim Rashid, Mathieu Lehanneur, Germain Bourré, and Nigel Coates.

Thanks to the Veuve Clicquot team in Reims and around the world; those who have in particular contributed to this book are Vanessa Kay, Elsa Corbineau and Genavieve Alexander, Virginie Bothua, Margaux Ollivier, Sylvie Felix, and Julien Bezançon.

This book is first and foremost a team effort, and it could not have happened without the extraordinary input of Catherine Bonifassi, managing editor; Duncan Campbell, art director, and Elena Luoto Meister, editor at large. My very special thanks to you three.

This book is dedicated to Seth Myron Stevens. Thank you for your support and advice.

The author's share of the profits on this book is donated to the Elton John AIDS Foundation, which dedicates 100 percent of the funds collected to fight AIDS around the world. If you wish to take part in this effort, please inquire at fundraising@ejaf.com.

PHOTO CREDITS

Slim Aarons/Getty Images: 78-79, 106

J.C. Amiel/Sucré Salé: 92

Germain Bourré: 127, 128

Luc Castel: 133

Michael Cole: 43

Tony Craddock/Bridge/Corbis: 138-139

Alfred Eisenstaedt/Time & Life Pictures/Getty Images: 76

Stéphane Feugère: 123, 134-135, 136-137, 171

foodanddrinkphotos co/Age Fotostock: 32

Robin Lynne Gibson/Stone/Getty Images: 167

Michel Guillard/Scope-Image: 18-19

Max von Gumppenberg & Patrick Bienert: 82, 84-85, 87, 140, 168, 169, 172-173, 174, 176-177, 179

Valery Hache/Getty Images: 162

Imagestate/Age Fotosock: 89

Dimitri Kessel/Time & Life Pictures/Getty Images: 46

Xavier Lavictoire: 67, 68-69, 70

Régine Mahaux: 54-55, 112-113, 116-117

Leonard McCombe/Time & Life Pictures/Getty Images: 152-153

Moët Hennessy Australia/Fiora Sacco: 77

Moët Hennessy España: 74-75, 180-181

Moët Hennessy Italy/Filippo Lambertenghi Deliliers: 52

Moët Hennessy Italy/Stefano Guindani: 120-121

Moët Hennessy UK: 144

Moët Hennessy UK/George Powell: 10-11, 47

Moët Hennessy USA: 146-147, 149, 150-151, 160-161

Genevieve Naylor/Corbis: 88

Bruno Peroussel/HOA-QUI/Gamma-Rapho: 81

Mickäel Russo: 44-45

Thibaut de Saint Chamas: 96-97

Slow Images/Getty Images: 13

Georgia Glynn Smith: 8, 28-29, 31, 34-35, 37, 38, 41, 48, 50-51, 57, 58-59, 60, 95, 98, 101, 102, 155, 156-157, 158

Jean-Daniel Sudres/Hemis.fr: 72

Pierre Terdjman: 27

Marie-José et Jean-François Tripelon/TOP/Gamma-Rapho: 91

William Vandivert/Time & Life Pictures/Getty Images: 132

Veuve Clicquot Archives: 6, 14-15, 16, 20, 23, 24, 25, 26, 62-63, 64, 104-105, 109, 110, 111, 114, 115, 124-125, 130, 131, 143, 164-165, 183

Veuve Clicquot Archives/Fabrice Bouquet: 119

The Veuve Clicquot international management team on the Chantilly polo field, 2010.